CAMP KNOCK KNOCK

CAMP KNOCK KNOCK

BETSY DUFFEY

ILLUSTRATED BY
FIONA DUNBAR

A Yearling First Choice Chapter Book

Published by
Bantam Doubleday Dell Publishing Group, Inc.
1540 Broadway
New York, New York 10036

Library of Congress Cataloging-in-Publication Data
The hardback of this title is cataloged as follows:
Duffey, Betsy.
Camp Knock Knock / by Betsy Duffey ; illustrated by Fiona Dunbar.
p.   cm.
"A Yearling First Choice Chapter Book"
Summary: Willie is king of the knock-knock jokes at summer camp, but
to retain his title he must win the great riddle contest against Crow,
who is best at everything.
ISBN 0-385-32190-2 (hardcover : alk. paper)—ISBN 0-440-41126-2 (pbk. : alk. paper)
[1. Jokes—Fiction.   2. Camps—Fiction.   3. Contests—Fiction.]
I. Dunbar, Fiona, ill.   II. Title.
PZ7.D876Cam   1996
[E]—dc20
95-619   CIP   AC

Hardcover: The trademark Delacorte Press® is registered in the U.S. Patent and
Trademark Office and in other countries.
Paperback: The trademark Yearling® is registered in the U.S. Patent
and Trademark Office and in other countries.
The text of this book is set in 17-point Baskerville.
Book design by Trish Parcell
Manufactured in the United States of America
July 1996
10 9 8 7 6 5 4 3 2

Contents

1. Food Fight

"Knock knock!"
Willie yelled.
"Who's there?"
the other kids yelled back.
They loved Willie's knock-knock jokes.

"Lettuce."

"Lettuce who?"

"Lettuce have a food fight!"

Slug threw some lettuce at Willie.

Willie ducked just in time.

Everyone laughed.

Mr. Harry blew his whistle.

"No food fights!" he said.

A pea hit Mr. Harry in the head.
He frowned.
"Do we throw food at camp?
Do we know how to behave?
Do we . . ."

No one was listening.

They were too busy throwing food.

"Willie," Slug said,

"you are the best.

You are the knock-knock king!"

9

"Not so fast," a voice said.

A big boy stood at the next table.

"I am Crow," he said.

"And I am the best at everything.
Who is best at basketball?"

"Crow!" the kids at his table yelled.

"And who can eat the most pie?"

"Crow!"

"And who won the egg toss?"

"Crow! Crow! Crow!"

"I am better at jokes," said Willie.

"No way!" Crow said.

"Let's have a contest," Slug said.

"You can each tell your best joke.

We will all decide on the winner."

Crow went first.

"Knock knock," he said.

"Who's there?" Willie asked.

"Little Old Lady."

"Little Old Lady who?"

"I didn't know you could yodel!"

The kids at Crow's table laughed.

"Got you!" Crow said. "Your turn."

"Knock knock," Willie said.

"Who's there?" Crow asked.

"Tank."

"Tank who?"

"You're welcome!" Willie said.

"Got you!" Willie's table yelled at Crow.

"It's a tie!" Slug said.

They all agreed.

"Let's go outside," said Crow.

"The contest has just begun!"

Everyone jumped up.

They ran to the door.

Mr. Harry blew his whistle.

"No running in the dining room!

Do we know how to behave?

Do we . . ."

No one was listening.

They were too busy running.

It was time for the contest.

2. The Contest

"Here are the rules," said Slug.
"We will walk across camp.
When we see a kid,
we will ask the kid's name.
Then you two will take turns.
You will tell jokes with the kids' names.
The first one to miss loses."
Crow and Willie walked across camp.
Everyone followed them.

PIGLET

They came to a girl paddling a boat.

Willie went first.

"What's your name?" he called.

"Mary," the girl called back.

Willie smiled. He turned to Crow.

"Knock knock," he said.

"Who's there?" Crow asked.

"Mary."

"Mary who?"

"Mary Christmas!"

Everyone giggled. Willie took a bow.

"Your turn," Slug said to Crow.

They saw a girl riding a horse.

"What's your name?" Crow called.

"Barbara," she said. Crow grinned.

"I know one," he said. "Knock knock."

"Who's there?" Willie asked.

"Barbara."

"Barbara who?"

"Barbara black sheep,
have you any wool?"

"Yay!" the kids yelled for Crow.

17

They came to a boy shooting arrows.

His name was Arch.

It was Willie's turn.

"Knock knock," Willie said.

"Who's there?" Crow asked.

"Arch."

"Arch who?"

"God bless you!"

All the kids laughed.

Crow even smiled a little.

They came to the crafts table.

A girl was making a basket.

"What's your name?" Crow asked.

"Annie."

"Knock knock," Crow said.

"Who's there?" Willie asked.

"Annie."

"Annie who?"

"Annie body home?"

The kids clapped.

Willie was next.

They saw a boy reading a book.

"What's your name?" Willie asked.

He hoped it would be Frank or Mike.

It was not Frank or Mike.

"Frederick Ornat," the boy said.

Slug said, "Uh-oh."

Crow said, "Great!"

Willie did not say a word.

He thought and thought.

For once he had no joke to tell.

3. Willie Make It?

"I win!" said Crow.

"I am the knock-knock king.

I am the best."

He danced and cheered.

"No fair," Willie said.

"Fair!" said Crow. He pointed at Slug.

"Your friend made the rules."

"Do I have to use
both names?" Willie asked.

"Yes!"

"First and last?"

"Yes," said Crow.

"He told you his name.

He could have just said Frederick.

That would have been hard.

But Frederick Ornat!"

Crow began to dance again.

"I am the winner!

I am the best! I am—"

"Not so fast," said Willie.

"Can't I have some

time to think?"

"I'll give you till campfire time."
Crow smiled.
"When Mr. Harry lights the fire, I win.
If you think of this one, I give up.
You win." Crow walked away.

It was a long day for Willie.
He walked to the lake
and sat under a tree.
He tried to think of his joke.
"Hey, Willie!" Crow called.
"Yeah?"
"Knock knock!"
"Who's there?"
"Willie."
"Willie who?"
"Willie make it?
Yuk yuk yuk," Crow laughed.

Willie went to the craft house.

He liked to think while he worked.

Willie worked on his key ring.

He tried to think of his joke.

"Hey, Willie," Crow called.

"Yeah?"

"Knock knock."

"Who's there?"

"Emma."

"Emma who?"

"Emma going to win!
Yuk yuk yuk!"

Willie hated the way Crow laughed.

There was one other place.

A place where he could think.

Willie got on top of his cabin.

He closed his eyes.

He tried to think of a joke.

"Knock knock."

Crow had found him.

"Who's there?" Willie asked.

"Boo."

"Boo who?"

"Are you crying

because you're losing?"

It was a long day for Willie.

Now he was not the knock-knock king.

The sun was going down.

It was almost campfire time.

Mr. Harry blew the whistle.

Everyone ran to the campfire circle.

Mr. Harry frowned.

He blew the whistle again.

"Do we run to the campfire?

Do we know how to behave?

Do we . . ."

No one answered.

They were too busy running.

Willie was the only one who walked.

4. Ready or Not!

The campers sat around a pile of wood.

Mr. Harry was coming to light the fire.

Willie looked across the pile of wood.

He could see Crow looking at him.

Crow smiled.

Willie did not smile back.

They heard the sound of a drum.

It was almost time.

Mr. Harry came into the circle.

Boom boom boom.

He beat the drum.

He held out a match.

"I am going to lose," Willie said.

"Maybe not," said Slug.

"You think," he said. "I'll stall."

Slug stood up. "Stop!" he yelled.

"Yes?" Mr. Harry said.

"I would like to sing a song."

"Okay," said Mr. Harry.

"But make it short."

"'Ninety-nine bottles

of pop on the wall . . . ,'"

Slug sang.

Willie thought.

Slug got down to eighty-five bottles.

Mr. Harry yelled, "Stop!"

"Don't you want to hear the rest?"
Slug asked.

"No! It is time for the campfire."

Boom boom boom.

Mr. Harry held out a match.

"Wait!" Slug yelled.

Mr. Harry frowned at Slug.

"What now?" he asked.

"I would like to say a poem."

"A poem?"

Mr. Harry did not look happy.

"Well," he said, "go ahead."

"'Twas the night before Christmas . . .'"

While Slug talked, Willie thought.

The poem was over too soon for Willie.

Boom boom boom.

Willie was out of time.

Mr. Harry lit the match.

He held it up.

Crow called out to Willie,

"Ready or not, here it comes!"

Willie's eyes opened wide.

"Stop!" he yelled. "Stop, Mr. Harry."

Mr. Harry turned.

"Now what?" he said.

"I would like to tell a joke," Willie said.

"A joke?"

"One small joke."

"Will it be short?"

"Yes."

Mr. Harry blew out the match.

"I give up," he said.

"Knock knock," said Willie.

"Who's there?" everyone yelled.

"Freddie Ornat."

"Freddie Ornat who?"

"Freddie Ornat, here I come!"

Crow hit his head with his hand.

Slug jumped up and down.

Mr. Harry shook his head.

Everyone yelled,

"You are the knock-knock king!

You are the best!"

They lifted Willie up.

They cheered and clapped.

Even Crow cheered.

Everyone cheered but Mr. Harry.

He was too busy packing up his drum.

5. Bye!

The last day of camp was here.

Crow had won the basketball shoot.

And the pie-eating contest.

And the egg toss.

But Willie was proud.

He was the knock-knock king.

For once he was the best!

Willie's father drove up.

He put Willie's things in the car.

Crow watched.

He was waiting for his parents too.

"Hey!" Crow called to Willie.

"Will you remember me in one week?"

"Sure!" said Willie.

"I'll never forget you!"

"Will you remember me
in one month?"

"Yes."

"Will you remember me in one year?"

"Of course!"

"Knock knock!"

"Who's there?"

"See," said Crow,

"you've forgotten me already!"

"Got you!" they both said together.

Willie got into the car.

He waved out the window.

"Bye!" he called to Slug.

Mr. Harry blew the whistle.

"Do we yell out of the car?

Do we know how to behave?

Do we . . ."

Willie was not listening.

He was too busy yelling out the window.

Willie had one more joke to tell.

"Knock knock," he yelled.

"Who's there?" Slug yelled back.

"Ozzie."

"Ozzie who?"

"Ozzie you next year!"

"You bet!"

About the Author

Betsy Duffey grew up in Morgantown, West Virginia, and spent many happy summer weeks at Camp Horseshoe in Elkins, West Virginia. She now lives in Atlanta with her husband and two sons. *Camp Knock Knock* is her fourteenth book for children.

About the Illustrator

Fiona Dunbar grew up in England, where she has illustrated many books for children and written three of her own. In 1993 she moved to New York, where she now lives with her husband and their daughter, Helena.